Marxism in America

Dr. John Mathew

(Sunny Ezhumattoor)

Marxism in America

Copyright © April 19, 2023, Dr. John Mathew

Published By
Thekkel Publications a
Division of Narrow Path Ministries
Web address: www.Thekkel.com
www.NarrowPathMinitries.net

All rights reserved. No portion of this book may be translated or reproduced in whole or in part in any form without the written permission of the author.

ISBN: 9798391933298

Table of Contents

Foreword

Introduction

Chapter One

Marxism in America   19

Chapter Two

Critical Race Theory
and Cancel Culture   39

Chapter Three

Climate Change   50

Chapter Four

Does Democratic Party Care
about Black People?   57

Chapter Five

Is Systemic Racism
Existing In America?   68

Bibliography   91

Foreword

My friend and well-known author of various Christian and secular books, Dr. Sunny Ezhumattoor had prepared this latest book, Marxism in America and is presenting it to his readers focusing on impending dangers the Unites States and the western world are now facing. At a time when technology and social media rule, the legacy of writers, authors, and poets remains vital. Their words and ideas continue to inspire us and shape our world, reminding us of the power of the written word and the importance of creativity, and imagination. A well written book can challenge our preconceived notions and beliefs by presenting alternative views and perspectives, which can make us rethink our own viewpoints. It can encourage us to think more deeply and critically about complex issues and themes, including inequality, and corruption. It allows us to experience the world through the eyes of others, including those from diverse cultures, backgrounds, and identities, which helps to cultivate greater empathy and understanding. Such books can inspire self-reflection and introspection, enabling us to identify our own biases and assumptions, and thus facilitating personal growth and development. They can serve as a catalyst for beneficial changes by exposing political injustices and prompt readers to think constructively. An informative book can offer a platform for marginalized voices to be heard, challenging dominant narratives, and amplifying the perspectives of those who have been silenced. The readers of this book are about to embark on a tumultuous journey through this and they may challenge the conventional wisdom of many, but those who voyage through it would find it very refreshing and revealing.

Political movements and organizations in the USA have been influenced by various ideologies, such as woke theory, critical race theory (CRT), and Marxism. These movements often seek to challenge the entrenched power dynamics in society and address issues related to systemic inequalities and discrimination. From a biblical perspective, there may be different appraisals of the role of these movements. On one hand, the Bible emphasizes the importance of social justice and caring for the poor and oppressed. In this sense, some of the expressed goals of these movements align with biblical values. But it vastly fails due to resorting to violence during its attempted implementation.

Upon careful analysis as the author had done, it proves that such affinity to these ideologies is based on flawed or warped understanding and can undermine the biblical values of freedom, individual responsibility, and respect for human dignity. He asserts that these movements often promote a victim mentality, negate personal agency, and ignore the complexity of human nature and social dynamics. The relationship between political movements and biblical values is complex and often produce unwarranted behavioral peculiarities in the society. While some of the goals of these movements align with biblical values, it is important to critically examine the paths taken to achieve such goals.

It is evident that the United States of America is experiencing a great divide amongst its people. Political and social differences have caused major divides and rifts among communities, leaving many feeling lost and hopeless. However, as a society, we must remember that we have a higher calling to aspire to. 2 Peter 1:3 "His divine power has given us all things that pertain to life and godliness through the knowledge of Him who called us by glory and virtue." Christians are to be the Ambassadors of such a higher calling. This should not be to promote divisive factions or to create an "us vs. them" mentality. Instead, it should be to love and serve one another as Jesus did. We must prioritize treating everyone with kindness and respect, regardless of their beliefs or backgrounds. Afterall, what we have in Christ including our faith in Him is a gift from above.

The author cites multiple examples and raises many red flags that the present generation needs to heed and the upcoming generation to cautiously avoid. He has warned us strongly through this book that lawlessness can have significant negative impacts on society. Also, he is marking out the damaging effects such as, the breakdown of institutions, an increase in violence and criminal activity, loss of trust, and the resulting economic collapse. A decisive turnaround coupled with absolute reliance upon the Lord, may help us regain much of the Judeo- Christian values, once the Unites States cherished but has lost lately. It is my desire that this book would spark the interest of several readers and achieve its intended goals.

Tom Johns,

Dallas, Texas

Introduction

Every generation must make a renewed defense of the true Gospel, because the Gospel is under attack in each successive generation. Wokeness, Transgenderism, and CRT are destroying the Christian foundation of America. The new idea is basically neo-Marxism for deconstruction and dismantling of Social and economic structures of the West. They have invented new vocabulary like systemic racism, implicit bias, whiteness, white privilege, cultural appropriation, colonization, microaggression, equity and social justice.

At the same time, Gospel doctrines like original sin, atonement, justification, and the glory of Christ are being eclipsed by new teaching with social inequalities, such as slavery, which can never be atoned by Biblical remedies. The only remedies are revenge and reparations. In many Black churches and liberal White churches, Gospel language is being supplanted by socialist sermons. They say that the American system is rooted in white supremacy and Western values. According to them every aspect of American culture is riddled with racism.

The liberals angrily state that the founders of America created the constitution, economic system, and civil societies for the benefit of the White race. Politicians, even conservative pastors, have no logical answers. Instead, they all blush and with a guilty face say that there is equality in America. Many White liberals agree with the angry Marxist Black activists. I consider that the accusations of the liberals about the injustices of the founding fathers are illogical, racists, in order to create division anger, jealousy, and hatred among some minorities who have no historical acumen.

We can find answers to most of the questions by using common sense with good knowledge of history. I would ask them like this, "How did Saudi Arabia establish their system? Did they pay attention to provide equal status to Shia Muslims and other minorities?" Yes, China made their system for their own people not for the benefit of India or any other countries.

White pilgrims, puritans and later other Europeans came to America and founded America. Hence making the system benefiting the White man is 100 percent appropriate. The liberals and other minorities must recognize that only American White people welcomed immigrants from 190 countries.

Now all immigrants are enjoying the fruits of the sacrifices of the founding population of America. On the other hand, no other Asian, Latin American, and African countries welcome foreigners. In some countries, if you cross the border illegally, the soldiers will shoot you on sight.

Liberals create a narrative in order to justify for an open border. They say Latin America is riddled with poverty and Crime. They are coming to America for a better living. However, they have not discovered the root problem. There are simple commonsense remedies for complex issues. South America is blessed with natural resources and paradise like natural beauty. They should be living like kings. I diagnose in one word the cause of their maladies. It is "Socialism" I also have a remedy in one word "Capitalism."

I attempted to exegete the relationship between religion and politics through a Biblical lens. This is a comprehensive guide for the 21 St century Christians on how to decipher the exact truth from a complex web of interpretations. I have written this book from the perspective of intense historical observation and Biblical studies for 65 years. We can glean great truths to guide us in every area of life.

2 Peter 1:3 states "His divine power has

given us everything needed for life and godliness, through the knowledge of Him who called us by His own glory and goodness."

My main purpose is not to explain the differences between the Republicans or Democrats, but to teach a biblical worldview and Biblical perspectives on politics, law and government. I do not have any preconceived notions about any of the previously mentioned issues. As Christians, we should be above race and nationality. When we die, we cease to be Anglo, Black, Hispanic, Indian, Asians, etc. Unfortunately, most Christians unknowingly subscribe to some tribal traits and practice eisegesis in interpreting the Bible and Socio- Political issues. There is no perfect people or party in the world. We Christians know that one day the perfect Jesus will rule the earth righteously. Today, even believers have the old nature. They never reach sinless perfection in this fallen world. We know that believers also lie and cheat, and are involved in quarrels, divisions, angry outbursts, gossiping, and jealousy.

The foundation of the Christian worldview is necessary in order to see the complete truth. As Christians, we must vote for the person or party who is aligned with the most Christian principles. We must always choose the lesser evil. Now many White mega church pastors have embraced BLM, CRT, LGBTIQ and Social Justice. Many people think that Socialism means Social Justice. I define Socialism like this **"A socialist is a Communist without guns and bombs."**

Historically, Indian Christians are aligned with the political left's Socialist ideology. Even after migrating to the USA, most Indian Christians only vote for the Democratic party. Some are spiritual leaders and elders who lead an exemplary Christian life. They raise their children imparting a great Biblical base. Many are involved in gospel work while doing secular jobs.

However, many Christian parents are not aware that they are raising Marxist serpents in their homes. I personally know some believers who gathered in the past in our Indian assembly who have children who are hardcore BLM supporters.

However, at the time of voting they vote for the party who introduced the same sex marriage and embrace terrorist groups like Antifa and BLM. They also teach that there are many dozens of genders and a man can become a woman and vice versa.

According to Kyle Morris and Sam Dorman of Fox news "More than 63 million abortions are estimated to have taken place in the U.S. since the Supreme Court's 1973 Roe v. Wade ruling that granted federal protections to women seeking to terminate their pregnancies, according to one analysis."

Many believers are confused and have asked me in great consternation why our young Indian Christians, like all other pagan Indians, support the Democratic party? My answer is reflected in the following story.

Then I narrate a fictious story which is prevalent in every culture with variations. I tell all my students and friends this story and ask them to internalize the great truth contained in this story. It may be the greatest story applicable in your life. Christians who embrace leftist ideology are making their reward in heaven null and void. At the Judgment Seat of Christ, if you did not vote based on Biblical values, all your sacrificial Christian life will be neutralized.

2 John 1:8 refers to a full reward:

"Watch out, so that you do not lose the things we have worked for, but receive a full reward."

The title of the story is Swimology. Do not be a Christian like this professor in the story. Try to *learn, read, understand, and think.*

The Young Professor and the old Layman

"On board of a big ship a simple old man met a young professor and they started to have conversations along the journey. Every night the man came to the professor's cabin, trying to learn something from the learned person. On the first night, the professor asked, 'Old man, do you know what Geology is?'

'Oh, Professor Sir, I never went to school, I know nothing about Geology. Could you tell me what it is?' replied the man.

'Oh, poor old man, you do not know what Geology is? It is the science of the earth. You have wasted a quarter of your life,' said the professor. The old man felt so sad. If the professor said that he wasted a quarter of his life, then it must be true.

On the second night, the two men met again, and the professor asked, 'Old man, do you know what Oceanology is?'

'Professor Sir, I am just a simple man, I do not know what Oceanology is. What is that sir?'

replied the old man. And the professor said, 'Oh, poor old man, you do not know what Oceanology is? We are sailing, and you do not know the science of the sea? You have wasted half of your life.' The old man felt so sad, so incredibly sad, for he just found out that he wasted half of his life.

On the third night, still eager to learn, the old man came to the professor's cabin and was asked, 'Old man, do you know what Meteorology is?'

'Professor Sir, you know I am just a simple man, I do not know what Meteorology is.' Replied the old man.

'Oh, poor old man, you do not know what Geology is; you also do not know what Oceanology is. And now you do not know what Meteorology is. Meteorology is the science of the sky and the weather. You have wasted three quarters of your life,' said the professor. The old man felt so sad, so incredibly sad, he just found out that he wasted three quarters of his life.

On the fourth night, the old man ran into the professor and started asking: 'Professor Sir, Professor Sir, do you know Swimology?'

'Old man, I know a lot of things, but I have never heard of Swimology. What is that?' replied the professor.

'Do you know how to swim, Sir?' Asked the old man.

'To swim? I did not have time to learn how to swim; I was busy learning other things. I cannot swim,' said the professor.

'Oh, poor Professor, you have wasted all your life. If you had known Swimology, you could swim to the shore, because the ship is sinking now,' said the old man.

I wish to thank several friends who helped me to complete this book. I want to thank Rob and Mary Terrill for their encouragement and assistance with my literature ministry. Sister Mary Terrill has edited most of my books. She has an eagle eye to find errors. She hails from an evangelist family and is a Bible teacher for Christian women.

Raymond Johnson, a missionary to Africa, is instrumental in publishing all my books on Amazon. I am deeply indebted to these believers who have a significant role in my literature ministry. I also thank Christian apologist Tom Johns for writing an appropriate foreword for this book. For the last forty years, believers all over the world have read my various books and many have been blessed. Ultimately, all glory goes to my Savior and Lord Jesus Christ who enabled me to write this.

1

Marxism in America

I had the privilege to come to America in the early 1970s. I am eternally grateful to my Lord and Savior, the Lord Jesus Christ, for enabling me to come to this great country. Just like other immigrants, I came for a better opportunity for myself and my future descendants. What makes it unique is my loyalty and devotion to America. Comparing other immigrants, I fell in love with America and its ideals, although it has blemishes just like any other nation. Many immigrated to America just to make money, without any intention to assimilate. Many are anti- Americans also. Recently I have been watching the gradual dismantling of America in front of my eyes. The Soviet Union tried to destroy America and made a major agenda to infiltrate the American educational system and media. However, the Socialist economic system became untenable and those who know history and logical thinking ignored it. Hence, the Soviet Union had a plan B which they started to implement in the 1930's. The main agenda was to implement and inject racial division. Their trump card had been to create enmity between the Black and White Race. The secular White also felt guilty about slavery and the injustice of the past. Since they are not Bible believing Christians most liberal Whites felt shame and guilt and they wanted to punish themselves for perceived redemption and supported the hidden Marxist agenda. Black Lives Matter started riots and property destruction all over America in 2019. If you watch the video clip you will be amazed to view the arson and looting which was conducted under the leadership of young White males and females.

There is a hidden reason for this behavior of the Leftists. Although the liberal Whites are angry, they have a subtle racism in their DNA. History would give all the answers. The Ku Klux Klan was founded by the Democratic party. They were the party of slave owners and oppressors. Although they feel guilty, they also feel that Blacks are inferior. Liberal Democrats think that Blacks need special protection because slavery created a psychological scar for them for generations. So, the White elites want to be the protectors of the Black race. On the other hand, conservatives believe that Blacks have the same intellect and abilities as the Whites, and if the society provides equal opportunity they can excel without any special protection. In sports, American Blacks excel more than anybody in the world. Also, America's Free Market system can help anyone who wants to excel. There are a dozen world renowned Black Economists in America. Thomas Sowell and Walter Williams are world renowned economists. In the seventies, when South Vietnam fell to the communists, hundreds of thousands of refugees came to America. They had no resources and did not know English. Many refugees also had no education. However, within two decades the whole Vietnamese community became affluent. America is the best country in the world for Blacks and other minority races.

When the Soviet Union collapsed, Communist China filled the gap and they are transforming American culture and Politics.

The liberals think that America cannot be improved, and they want to destroy our existing system. They want to create a new America which will be free of poverty, racism, White Supremacy, and inequality. They believe they can remake a new Utopian America.

Karl Marx Vision of Socialist Supremacy

The Leftist social warriors want to introduce sexually explicit curriculum in schools and teach the equality as embracing the concept of LGBTQ. They also teach that the White race is evil, and they cause all the problems in the world. The agenda is called "Critical Race theory". Also, they want to erase the distinctions between male and female.

Karl Marx introduced a theory of Socialist supremacy. After the Bolshevik Revolution in 1917 by Vladimir Lenin, it was necessary to introduce economic and social controls, during which millions of people were killed. The state abolished private property and set out to bring "equality and justice" to an oppressed people. The state suppressed religion and freedom of speech.

Today, our life is replete with cultural Marxism. It is not being imposed on people by force; instead, it is a subtle and attractive form of Marxism that wins the hearts and minds of people incrementally by the gradual transformation of the culture. Bombarded with exaggerated and illusionary promises, people accept it because they are convinced of its benefits. It promises "Hope and Change" income equality, racial justice, and justice based on progressive values rather than bigoted religious morality.

(One classic example is the broken promises of Obama care which occurred at least twenty-three times between 2008 and 2010. New York Magazine has put together a video of President Obama promising Americans if they like their doctor or like their healthcare plan, they could keep it...which we have found out is not the case for most Americans.)

Cultural Marxists seek to capture five cultural institutions: The Social, Political, educational, religious, and family.

The Destruction of the Nuclear Family

I am quoting from the original Manifesto of the Communist party by Karl Marx and Frederick Engels. Printed by Progress Publishers Moscow 1965 Page 67

"Abolition of the family!" Even the most radical flare up at this infamous proposal of the communists.

On what foundation is the present family, the bourgeois family, based? On capital, on private gain. In its completely developed form this family exists only among the bourgeoisie. But this state of things finds its complement in the practical absence of the family among the proletarians, and in public prostitution.

The bourgeois family will vanish as a matter of course when its complement vanishes, and both will vanish with the vanishing of capital.

Do you charge us with wanting to stop the exploitation of children by their parents? To this crime we plead guilty.

But you will say, we destroy the most hallowed of relations, when we replace home education with social.

And your education! Is not that also social, and determined by the social conditions under which you educate, by the intervention, direct or indirect, of society, by means of school, etc.? The Communists have not invented the intervention of society in education; they do but seek to rescue education from the influence of the ruling class. The bourgeois clap trap about the family and education, about the hallowed co- relation of parent and child, becomes all the more disgusting, the more by the action of Modern Industry, all family ties among the proletarians are torn asunder, and their children transformed into simple articles of commerce and instruments of labor.

"But you Communists would introduce the community of women," screams the whole bourgeoisie in chorus.

The bourgeois sees in his wife a mere instrument of production. He hears that the instruments of production are to be exploited in common, and, naturally, can come to no other conclusion than that the lot of being common to all will likewise fall to the women.

He has not even a suspicion that the real point aimed at is to do away with the status of women as mere instruments of production.

For the rest, nothing is more ridiculous than the virtuous indignation of our bourgeois at the community of women which, they pretend, is to be openly and officially established by the Communists. The Communists have no need to introduce the community of women; it has existed almost from time immemorial.

Our bourgeois, not content with having the wives and daughters of their proletarians at their disposal, not to speak of common prostitutes, take the greatest pleasure in seducing each other's wives.

Bourgeois marriage is in reality a system of wives in common and thus, at the most, what the Communists might possibly be reproached with, is that they desire to introduce, in substitution for a hypocritically concealed, an openly legalized community of women. For the rest, it is self-evident that the abolition of the present system of production must bring with it the abolition of the community of women springing from that system, i.e., of prostitution both public and private.

The Communists are further reproached for desiring to abolish countries and nationality.

In proportion, as the exploitation of one individual by another is put an end to, the exploitation of one nation by another will also be put an end to.

Joseph Biden became the 46th president of USA on January 20, 2021. His administration opened the Southern Border. Ever since close to 200,000 illegals per month are entering the USA from more than 100 countries. Marxism is in action in America.

Standing in the way of these changes is the nuclear family with a father, a mother, and children. Marx taught that families based on natural law and Judeo- Christian values breed inequality and feed on greed and systemic oppression. Such families had to be dismantled if the Marxist vision of equality was to be realized. Marx taught that the restrictions limiting sexual intimacy to a one-man one-woman relationship within the marriage covenant were invented by religion to maintain the dominance of men. Marxists believe one of the benefit of mothers joining the workforce is that their children must then attend state-sponsored daycare centers and schools where they can be taught about the errors of Creationism and the Bible. Children can also be indoctrinated about the evils of capitalism and the benefits of Socialism to bring economic equality. For this to become a reality, the education of children must be taken out of the hands of the parents and surrendered to the state.

Victimology

We all know that poverty, inequality, and injustice exist all over the world. Marxists are experts of exploiting the real grievances of downtrodden people. Women are told they are victims of the past, and still victims of the present social and religious systems under men. To implement the force of victimology, liberals are rewriting the American history by mere fabrication.

Hardcore Marxist Saul Alinsky 's theories had great influence on Hillary Clinton and Barak Hussain Obama. Alinsky is the author of the book "Rules for Radicals" which he dedicated to "Lucifer... the first radical who rebelled against the establishment and did it so effectively that he at least won his own

Kingdom." (Saul D. Alinsky. Rules for Radicals: A pragmatic Primer for Realistic Radicals [New York: Vintage Books, 1989, ix.])

Here is another statement of Alinsky: "An organizer must stir up dissatisfaction and discontent. He must create a mechanism that can drain off the underlying guilt for having accepted the previous situation for so long time. Out of this mechanism, a new community organization arises." (Alinsky, Rules for Radicles, 117.)

Communists and dictators have different meanings for every word. For example, Adolf Hitler's concentration camps were described as freedom camps. North Korea and Communist China are called the People's Republic.

The purpose of propaganda is to change people's perception of reality. Despite real counter evidence, people will not change their minds. Alinsky saw the conflict among people are not only economics alone. He wanted to perpetuate the main conflicts in America based on race. Racism would be used to ferment the revolution in America. Communism is implemented with various other names. It is rebranded in America as social justice, political correctness, diversity, and equality. Today the word equality is applied to every social cause imaginable. They define marriage equality to promote same sex marriage, economic equality to promote Socialism, reproductive equality to promote abortion, healthcare equality to promote free socialized health care, gender equality to promote transgender ideology, etc.

However, the Bible teaches equal responsibility based on the gifts and talents we are given.

Propaganda

What has been is what will be, and what has been done is what will be done, and there is nothing new under the sun. (Ecclesiastes 1:9)

The origin of the fake news

The fake news originated immediately after the resurrection of the Lord Jesus Christ by Jewish leaders of Israel. Since 1980s the American media and American corporations owned by liberal Jews reignited the same type of fake news in political, economic, and social areas. It is amazing to know that even today, if you ask any Jewish person most of them may repeat the 2000-year-old story of the stolen body of Jesus. In Matthew 28:11-15 we read,

"Now while they were going, behold, some of the guard came into the city and reported to the chief priests all the things that had happened. When they had assembled with the elders and consulted together, they gave a large sum of money to the soldiers, saying, 'Tell them, "His disciples came at night and stole Him away while we slept." And if this comes to the governor's ears, we will appease him and make you secure.' So, they took the money and did as they were instructed; and this saying is commonly reported among the Jews until this day."

Fake news—news articles, Television and radio programs that are intentionally and verifiably false designed to manipulate people's perceptions of reality—have been used to influence politics and promote the agenda of certain groups. Both Left and Right use this tool for their own benefits. But it has also become a method to stir up and intensify social, racial, and economic conflicts. Stories that are untrue and that intentionally mislead readers have caused growing mistrust among American people. In some cases, this mistrust resulted in violent protest over imaginary events, or violence. This unravels the fabric of American life, turning neighbor against neighbor. Why would anyone do this? People, organizations, and governments—foreign governments and even our own—use fake news for two different reasons. First, they intensify social and racial conflicts to undermine people's faith in the democratic process and people's ability to work together. Second, they distract people from important issues so that these issues remain unresolved.

Following the Nazi obtained power in 1933, Hitler established a Reich Ministry of Public Enlightenment and Propaganda headed by Joseph Goebbels. The Ministry's aim was to ensure that the Nazi message was successfully communicated through art, music, theater, films, books, radio, educational materials, and the press.

There were several audiences for Nazi propaganda. Germans were reminded of the struggle against foreign enemies and Jewish subversion. During periods preceding legislation or executive measures against Jews, propaganda campaigns created an atmosphere tolerant of violence against Jews, particularly in 1935 (before the Nuremberg Race Laws of September) and in 1938 (prior to the barrage of antisemitic economic legislation following Kristallnacht). Propaganda also encouraged passivity and acceptance of the impending measures against Jews, as these appeared to depict the Nazi government as stepping in and "restoring order."

Real and perceived discrimination was against ethnic Germans in east European nations which had gained territory at Germany's expense following World War 1, such as Czechoslovakia and Poland, was the subject of Nazi propaganda. This propaganda sought to elicit political loyalty and so-called race consciousness among the ethnic German populations. It also sought to mislead foreign governments—including the European Great Powers—that Nazi Germany was making understandable and fair demands for concessions and annexations.

After the German invasion of the Soviet Union, Nazi propaganda linked Soviet Communism to European Jewry. Hitler presented Germany as the defender of "Western" culture against the "Judeo-Bolshevik threat," and painting an apocalyptic picture of what would happen if the Soviets won the war. This was particularly the case after the catastrophic German defeat at Stalingrad in February 1943. These themes may have been instrumental in inducing Nazi and non-Nazi Germans as well as local collaborators to fight on until the very end".

Films played an important role in disseminating racial antisemitism, the superiority of German military power, and the intrinsic evil of the enemies as defined by Nazi ideology. Nazi films portrayed Jews as "subhuman" creatures infiltrating Aryan society. For example, The Eternal Jew (1940), directed by Fritz Hippler, portrayed Jews as wandering cultural parasites.

George Orwell's Novel *1984*

In the novel *1984*, we can read the description of a shocking totalitarian state, how the so- called Ministry of Truth used a subtle sinister language, Newspeak, to brainwash the people. The slogan was "War is Peace; freedom is slavery; ignorance is strength." Slavery to the state was presented as the gateway to freedom and prosperity. Conquest was sold as liberation.

George Orwell offered insights that all of us must read:

"The purpose of propaganda is to change people's perception of reality so that despite compelling counterevidence, people will not change their minds. The goal is to make people impervious to facts, scientific proof, and common sense."

In April 2022, Homeland Security Secretary Alejandro Mayorkas testified that a Disinformation Governance Board had recently been created days after Tesla CEO Elon Musk purchased Twitter, to combat online disinformation and would be led by undersecretary for policy Rob Silvers and principal deputy general counsel Jennifer Gaskill. After public outcry they postponed the formation of the board. Only the power of propaganda can account for movement that clamor for defunding the police and vilify law enforcement officers as a great threat to our society, at the same time encouraging the destruction of cities by anarchists.

Hitler used slogans to mask the evil. The extermination of the Jews was called "cleansing the land." Euthanasia was referred to as "the best of modern therapy." When Hitler starved children, he called it "putting them on a low – calorie diet."

"A woman's right to choose." Choose what? The full sentence is like this: "A woman's right to kill her own baby."

When the liberals perform atrocious acts, they would say it is for the good of the society.

A classical historical proof is given by former Moody Bible college president Erwin W. Lutzer in his book, *We Will not be Silenced* by Harvest House Publishers, Eugene Oregon. Page 130

"As an example, let us consider how a tobacco company convinced women that they should smoke and do so in public. Until about 1926, it was considered improper for women to smoke publicly. George Washington Hill's American Tobacco Company (which included the brand Lucky Strike) hired Edward Bernays to change this unwanted impediment to their business. If they could convince women to smoke openly, they might almost double their business.

Bernays, who combined his philosophy of propaganda with psychology and was the nephew of Sigmund Freud, came up with an ingenious idea: Remind women that they are oppressed, and call cigarettes their "torches of freedom."

In 1929, they gathered a group of women who marched in Network's Easter Sunday parade while smoking, proudly displaying their "torches of freedom." For women, smoking publicly now became a symbol of nonconformity, independence, and strength. It was a sign of rebellion against male dominance.

Any cause can have a legitimate appeal if it is tied to some noble idea. Even evil, if packaged correctly, can appear to be good, and good can be packaged as evil. Isaiah 5:20 says "Woe to those who call evil good and good evil; who put darkness for light, and light for darkness; who put bitter for sweet, and sweet for bitter."

This is how gay lifestyle became gay pride.

Saul Alinsky

Hillary Clinton and Barack Hussain Obama received inspiration from Saul Alinsky. Hillary Clinton, in 1969, chose her thesis on Saul Alinsky for the Bachelor of Arts degree program, at Wellesley College, Massachusetts.

Barack Obama was trained by Alinsky's disciples when he was a community organizer in Chicago in the mid-to-late 1980's. He was supported by 20 Protestant churches in the area.

Saul Alinsky, the hardcore Marxist, wrote in his book *Rules for Radicles* on page 36:

"The tenth rule of the ethics of means and ends is that you do what you can with what you have and cloth it with moral garments. In the field of action, the first question that arises in the determination of means to be employed for particular ends is what means available."

What Does the *"End Justifies the Means"* Mean?"

This phrase is used as an excuse to achieve their goals through any means necessary, no matter how immoral or illegal the means may be. It usually involves doing something wrong to achieve a positive end and justifying the wrongdoing by pointing to a good outcome.

I believe that all the writers up to this day are wrong in giving the credit of this famous quote to Niccolò Machiavelli. Really this credit must be awarded to Muhammad and Allah. His followers copied the so-called divine revelation of Allah to Muhammad. The Koran and Islam promote lying and cheating to attain the goal of Islam. When anyone picks up the Bible, they are almost immediately confronted with the fact that Satan is the greatest deceiver. Allah brags by calling himself Khayrul-Makireen, which literally means the "Greatest of all Deceivers." (Quran 3:54)

In America, liberals follow these principles. Hitler, Mao, and all the evil tyrants practiced it. Communism practices it. How is it in the Bible it is the devil and his henchman the Anti-Christ that are respectably referred to as the schemers, liars, and the deceivers, but in the Quran, it is Allah who is the greatest of all deceivers.?

2

Critical Race Theory and Cancel Culture

The transcript is taken from the online YouTube video program by Raymond Johnson on March 23, 2021 "Light from the Word" Critical Race Theory, Cancel Culture. Video # 44

Francis Schaeffer described how ideas escape the ivory towers of universities and Think Tanks, eventually to shape how ordinary people think, speak, and view their world. In 2020, one idea made that journey in record time. The Critical Race Theory or CRT, once relegated to academic papers and classroom discussions, has become everyday word in our lives. The CRT offers a diametrically opposite view that is consistent with Biblical values. The CRT describes who we are, and what is wrong with the world, and prescribes solutions that are opposite to Biblical principles. Many people of goodwill desire to combat injustice, eradicate racism, and climate oppression. George Santayana, a Spanish philosopher, stated, "Those who forget history are doomed to repeat it." American culture over the past 75 years has become less literate and has forgotten the lessons of the past while calling others "ignorant." Consequently, when the ideas from the "old serpent" repackaged for today are presented, they are accepted because they sound good to the unlearned ear, or in Rush Limbaugh's words 'Low Information crowd." Many Christians embraced the intersectionality train unaware that it leads to a catastrophic crash. Intersectionality is the concept that all oppression is linked. A group of marginalized people are victims. CRT is a worldview that divides humanity into two competing tribes: the oppressor and the oppressed. The oppressor is anyone who has a real or perceived advantage over others. Karl Marx similarly divided humanity into two groups: Bourgeoisie or Capitalist and the Proletariat or working class. The CRT or intersectionality teaches that the powerful always oppress the powerless. Consequently, the oppressed possess a greater degree of moral superiority. The oppressors have become numb to the plight of the oppressed. The oppressors or White men are ignorant and clueless to the plight of the oppressed. It is their social DNA. People may belong to more than one oppressed group. Here is a short list of the oppressors: Heterosexuals, Whites, Males, and Europeans. Oppressed: Gays and lesbians, transgender, Blacks, females, and other people of color. A White heterosexual male would be the proto-oppressor or the arche-type oppressor. He would have the least amount of moral authority as well as the greatest amount of moral responsibility because he is part of an oppressive tribe that has mistreated others down through the ages. When speaking on matters of race or culture, the White heterosexual male must shut up and listen as his comeuppance. A Black heterosexual male would have more moral authority because, being black, he is a member of two oppressed groups. Individuality is lost within the group you belong to. If you try to defend yourself, it proves that you are a racist. Wealthy Black Americans are not considered privileged, but a White person born into abject poverty is considered a person of privilege. Salvation, in the radical view of CRT, is to gain power over your oppressors. The Bible frames human life through the lens of Adam vs Christ, placing all members of society into one of these two groups; children of God and the children of the devil (1 John 3:10). All people are God's creation (Colossians 1:16). Only those who are born again are children of God (John 1:12 and Romans 8:16).

The CRT sees the world culminating toward a utopia based on deconstruction of oppressed systems. They believe that White people execute their power by systematic control over legal, cultural, and institutional structures that define civilization. These structures must be removed. "Defund the Police" is the first step, because White people benefit from these systems of oppression. They are blinded by their prejudice and subconscious bias against racial minorities. White people enter the world as oppressors and racial minorities enter the world as oppressed.

For a Christian, God is the standard for all objective truth. Truth cannot be subjective. All men enter the world in their default position in Adam, who is in active rebellion against God (Romans 5:12). God did not create race. The color of Adam's skin was irrelevant. Because all humans are equally created in God's image, all humans are equally worthy of dignity, honor, and respect.

Woke - Video # 44

We have always assumed the word woke is the past tense or past participle of wake - the state of being awake after sleeping.

Before 2014, the call to "Stay Woke" was unheard of. It originated in 2014 after the police killing of Michael Brown in Ferguson, Missouri. "Stay Woke" became a watch word for the Black Lives

Matter Movement. It meant keeping watch for police brutality. Christianity and CRT are two opposing worldviews. CRT sees salvation as social liberation, activism, and protest. It insists on penance, reparation a comeuppance. It is a woke salvation devoid of grace. As a result of these fatal flaws, CRT makes a wrong diagnosis and prescribes a deadly poison. A new order with mankind can only start with a new life through Christ changing us from the inside out (2 Corinthians 5:17). Many Americans have a narrow view of the world problems. They think that if they can resolve the problems in America, then the rest of the world would automatically reform in issues such as climate change and racism.

One of the consequences of these atheist systems is the collapse of English – speaking nations.

Before the Rapture, we can see the collapse of America and Europe.

CRT, BLM, Antifa, and Woke are the final blow to Western democracies. For several years wokeness has been changing the landscape of the church in North America. Cambridge Dictionary defines Woke as "A state of being aware, especially of social problems such as racism and inequality"- which sounds righteous. The urban dictionary gives another definition:

> On the surface Wokeness sounds like a noble cause. Being alerted to injustices around us should always be a good thing. In 2013, the Black Lives Matter Movement began as a reaction to police brutality against the Black community. In the Woke system, there is no grace and love, only retribution. The main BLM activist Ashleigh Shackelford, standing before a room of women (most of them White) told them, "All White people are racists. They have no chance of changing. No, you are always going to be racists." She also added, "I believe all White people are born into not being human." Her final verdict was, "White people grow up to be demons."

Liberal Remedies

According to liberal theology, a White housewife can address her sins and become an antiracist. Beneficiaries of "Whiteness" must identify themselves as racists and embrace a kind of secular conversion experience that is often marked by a public declaration. They can become an anti - racist through confession and conversion.

Woke Church

Eric Mason, Woke Church (2018)

Eric Mason is the founding pastor of "Epiphany Fellowship" in Philadelphia, Pennsylvania. In Mason's 2018 book, "Woke Church", he argues that "the essence of wokeness means holding White people accountable for the racial injustice we are entrenched in. White people have created a privileged system of institutions and structures of oppression."

The Biblical Outlook for a Christian

The first Biblical words about humans define the first man and woman in theological terms. Humanity is the creation of God; man is not an evolved product of other creatures but is made by God. (Genesis 2:7,22). Our skin color is part of the beautiful diversity of God. There is only one race. Every person is an image bearer, but no one is an end unto themselves. The Lord Jesus Christ is the last Adam and the second Man. Ephesians chapter 2 describes our previous and present conditions. In Ephesians 2:19-20, Paul used the illustrations of a fellowship a family, through Christ. Gentiles were strangers and aliens from the commonwealth of Israel. Now through Christ, Gentiles are fully integrated into the body of Christ. Paul described the Church as a glorious building that rests on a magnificent foundation, Christ, and His apostles. The apostles and prophets completed their foundation building job in the first century when they wrote the New Testament and shared it with the world. The Church no longer needs apostles and prophets. Woke is a do-it-yourself Christianity. Ethnicity is a vehicle by which God communicates in visible form, the uniqueness and brilliance of the Gospel. His people have unity in diversity. We can see an ethnic dispute in Acts 6: "Then the elders appointed deacons, seven Godly men were chosen." There were no reparations or retribution. Instead of going nuclear or embracing Marxism, we should go to Scripture to find a solution. Vivek Ramaswamy, the famous author of Woke Inc., states, "Why I am defecting? I am fed up with corporate America's game of pretending to care about justice in order to make money."

Today's American values are in the hands of a small group of Capitalists rather than American citizens. Wokeness has remade American capitalism in its own image. Basically, being Woke means obsessing about race, gender, and sexual orientation. Climate change is their new religion. If you want to get a job, you must believe in woke capitalism. When companies use their market power to make moral rules, they effectively prevent those other citizens from having the same say in our democracy. CEO's tell employees what they are supposed to think about moral questions. Wokeness sacrifices true diversity of thought, so that skin deep symbols of diversity, like race, and gender can thrive. Wokeness is diametrically opposite to Christianity. Wokeness separates people according to Whiteness, which is an unbiblical concept. Wokeness does not tackle the sin problem. Wokeness gives approval to evil- both in the public realm and in rejecting God's design for the sexes. Wokeness creates an alternative truth. In Ephesians 2:12-16, Paul has a burden to reveal where true unity is found. His letter is addressed to the Ephesian Christians, who had a Gentile background. He points to the stark covenantal division between the Gentiles and the Jews. In Galatian 3:28 we read "There is no longer Jew or Gentile, slave or free, male, or female. For you are all one in Christ Jesus."

At the Rapture, the Woke church will be left out. The false prophet will become the head and he will cancel all other faiths. Cancel culture is the beginning of that Antichrist system. In Revelation chapters 17 and 18 we can see the ultimate fulfillment of the CRT and cancel culture.

Social Justice. 12-7-2020

This transcript is taken from the online YouTube video program #31 by Raymond Johnson on December 9, 2020 "Light from the Word" Biblical and Social Justice.

The word "Social Justice" is a magical word for political progressives and young Christian believers. The concept of fairness, social justice, and equality can be seen in Genesis 3:1-4. "The serpent was the shrewdest of all the wild animals the Lord God had made. One day he asked the woman, "Did God really say you must not eat the fruit from any of the trees in the garden?"

"Of course, we may eat fruit from the trees in the garden," the woman replied. "It's only the fruit from the tree in the middle of the garden that we are not allowed to eat. God said, 'You must not eat it or even touch it; if you do, you will die.'"

"You won't die!" the serpent replied to the woman. "God knows that your eyes will be opened as soon as you eat it, and you will be like God, knowing both good and evil."

In verse 4, we can see the serpent is advising Eve how to become equal to God. This concept became an organized force in the nineteenth century with the birth of Socialism and Communism. Recently, the Social Justice movement added many contemporary issues to include, climate change, racial inequality, free healthcare, free housing, basic level of monthly income, and LGBTQ (Lesbian, Gay, Bisexual, Transgender, and Queer) rights.

If you read the Communist Manifesto, or the manifesto of the Bolshevik Revolution, you will see the exact copy of the economic agenda of the Democratic party. The latest additions are B.L.M and Antifa. Antifa means: Anti-fascist, which sounds peace loving. This name is reminiscent of the names of some Communist countries such as the People's Republic of China, and peoples Republic of Korea etc. BLM and Antifa want to punish the White race for their past sins. In my study and observations, I am convinced of one fact: Indians and American Blacks are the most racist people under the sun. American Blacks are still behaving like African tribes.

3
Climate Change

Only a few people on the globe know how global warming became climate change. Most people are not aware that the United Nations and the American government provide huge financial incentives for the scientists who support global warming. When logically - thinking people began to question the veracity of global warming, they subtly changed to Climate Change theory. The Leftists use this technique in every aspect of their lives.

In 1967, the Los Angeles Times carried a story headlined "Dire Famine Forecast by 1975." The story said it might "already be too late."

On August 10, 1969, the New York Times quoted a 37-year-old scientist predicting a new Ice Age and that "everyone will disappear in a cloud of blue steam by 1989."

An April 16, 1970, a story in the Boston Globe quoted Dr. Paul R. Erlich of the University of California, Riverside, predicting that America will be "subject to water rationing by 1974 and food rationing by 1980."

Paul Ehrlich predicted in 1970, "Between 1980 and 1989, some 4 billion people, including 65 million Americans, would perish in the "Great Die-off."

On July 9, 1971, The Washington Post, which, like most other media, now claims climate change and a warming planet is "settled science." It quoted Dr. S.I. Rasool of NASA and Columbia University. Rasool predicted a coming "new ice age." He was described as a "leading atmospheric scientist," so he should be believed. He predicted we had only about "50 or 60 years" to save ourselves from freezing to death.

Al Gore predicted in 2006 "Humans may have only ten years left to save the planet from turning into a total frying pan."

Alexandria Ocasio-Cortez predicted in 2019, "The world is going to end in 12 years if we don't address Climate Change."

The Democratic party leader and California congressman claimed more than three years that he had clear evidence to prove Trump's illegal collusion with Russia in the 2016 election. After intense investigation by special prosecutor Robert Muller, President Trump was exonerated. Muller and his attorneys were rabid Anti- Trump lawyers. Although they tried, they could not find anything to charge President Trump. However, Adam Schiff never apologized. It is interesting to read his tweet on Climate Change:

"We have a narrow window to act on climate change before it's too late. And that window is closing rapidly. History will not be kind to those who stand in the way of action. If there is anyone left to write it."5:16 PM Jul 16, 2022

"If you go back to Time Magazine, they actually were proclaiming the next Ice Age is coming, now it's become global warming... How do you believe the same people that were predicting just a couple decades ago that the new Ice Age is coming?" (Sean Hannity).

Even if the USA eliminates all cars, planes, and factories, it is not going to help the world climate. There are some huge pollutants in the world. Russia has the area of 6.6 sq. mi, China's area is 4 million SM, Canada 3.8 SM, India 1.2 million SM, Brazil 3 million SM, and Australia close to 3 million SM. All the climate doom for the last 50 years has failed. The Leftist climate expert and respected Democratic party Congress woman Alexandria Ocasio- Cortez in a news conference on January 22,

2019, warned that the world is going to end in 12 years. The readers can google and find out her academic background. Another Social Justice group called "Cancel Culture" became prominent in 2015. Whoever speaks against climate change or Social Justice will be silenced or cancelled.

Social Justice and Socialism

Socialism is the biggest lie of the 20th century. However, they are truthful in implementing their promises. The most important slogan of Social Justice is the elimination of income inequality. Yes, they have fulfilled that one promise in all Communist countries for the last 100 years. Everyone in Communist countries became equally poor and shared their miseries equally. Former British Prime minister Margaret Thatcher stated, "Socialism will run smoothly for the initial few years until all the money is gone." If we (America) confiscated 100 percent of the wealth of Jeff Bezos, Elon Musk, Bill Gates, Warren Buffet, Mark Zuckerberg, and other billionaires, we would have enough money to run the Federal government for 8 months. A Ponzi scheme or chain letter initially succeeds, but eventually collapses. A Pyramid scheme is ultimately unsustainable because it is based on faulty principles. In Socialist countries one person may be confiscating all the wealth. What if 51 percent of misguided Americans vote to confiscate all the wealth. Is it right? No more so than if one person robbed their property. The result or effect is the same for the victim. Under Socialism, a few people controlled the means of production. Under Capitalism people controlled the means of production. If you prefer a Lexus, Lincoln Continental, Cadillac to a Mercedes Benz, Porsche, or Bentley, or maybe an iPhone to the Samsung Galaxy, you don't have to elect a person. You do it directly by paying for them. Here we see the secret of how those billionaires like Elon Musk, Jeff Bezos, Steve Jobs, and Larry Ellison became rich: we made them rich. The inequality that Socialists complain about is the result of popular mandate. Free Markets work by satisfying our wants and the most successful businesspeople are those who anticipate our wants even before we have them. No one wrote to Steve Jobs beforehand to make a phone that could email, take photos, had a GPS, was able to stream movies, etc. He conceived it and built it before we knew we could not live without it. Capitalism itself is a form of Social Justice. The Socialist system is built upon the immorality of theft. Take from one to give to another. Socialism is unnatural. All things in nature are Capitalistic. Can I tell the oak tree in my front yard how much water and nutrients it can take from the soil? Can I control the squirrel in my front yard, how many acorns it can eat? All the living creatures work to produce a profit on their labors for their future. Capitalism may leave a few lazy people at the bottom. Still, Capitalist Western countries help them to be sustainable. Western governments have provisions to take care of physically and mentally challenged people. We can call it compassionate capitalism. However, Socialism leaves everyone at the bottom. In an ideal utopian world, Socialism would be the best economic system: However, we forget that all humans are deprived in this fallen sinful world. Self-interest is a God given virtue to survive in this world. Consider a college classroom: students work hard to pass the examination. The fruits of their labor can be seen in their grades. Suppose the professor were to say on the first day of class that to be fair and promote social justice, he would assign grades by taking the average of the class and giving each the same grade. In an ideal world, all would study hard for the sake of learning and to boost the overall average we understand, no student would study at all, because no matter how hard he or she worked, there would be no payoff of a higher grade. The hardest working students would complain bitterly about the professor's grading method and probably drop the course. In this same way, Socialism fails. In its pursuit of ideals and noble goals of equality and justice, its complete lack of incentives ignores the basic human nature. Self-interest is the motivating factor of all human activities. The success of Capitalism lies in the fact that it recognizes the inherent human greed in all of us and harnesses it for the economic good of all. Students who study hard to get better jobs with higher pay, entrepreneurs who start businesses to make themselves more prosperous, and investors who create new products that improve the quality of life for humanity are driven by their desire for more wealth. Poverty and economic injustice exist because capitalism is not being applied rigorously or properly, not because of it. The best example was in the 2008 financial crisis: the governmental intervention from Jimmy Carter to Bill Clinton caused that crisis. The collapse of the sub-prime loan had a domino effect and created a chain reaction in the global economy.

4

Does the Democratic Party Care about Black People?

Most people in America, especially black people, believe that the Democratic party cares about all minorities, especially black people. From history we know that only a few scholars understand the sinister plot of some elite politicians. After the Civil War, the White racists established the Ku Klux Klan. They wanted to exterminate the Black race in America. They were against all minorities. I am not going to provide the details of their atrocities. Any reader can access it. Most people do not know that the Klan was established by the Democratic party. Over the years, the White racists could not do those atrocities. After the Second World War, society in America began to change. Hence, the White racist began to change their policies in a subtle way. They believed that the Black people were inferior, and they needed special protection to advance in the society.

After the assassination of President Kennedy, Lyndon Johnson became president.

Johnson is known as the champion of the "Civil Rights Acts of 1964." This act eliminated all discrimination against Blacks and gave them special assistance and privileges. They did not do this out of compassion; however, it was a political stunt to get Black votes. Today, more than 90 percent of Blacks vote for the Democratic party. Without much explanation, an intelligent reader can understand the sinister plot of the Democratic party.

President Lyndon Johnson's Conversation About Black People

Here is a quotation by Lyndon Johnson taken from the post by David Emery, "These Negroes, they are getting pretty uppity these days and that's a problem for us since they've got something now, they never had before, the political pull to back up their uppityness. Now we have got to do something about this, we've got to give them a little something, just enough to quiet them down, not enough to make a difference. For if we don't move at all, then their allies will line up against us and there'll be no way of stopping them, we'll lose the filibuster and there'll be no way of putting a brake on all sorts of wild legislation. It will be Reconstruction all over again." President B. Lyndon Johnson once said, "I'll have those niggers voting Democratic for 200 years."

But there were also instances of casual racism that can't be so easily rationalized. Biographer Caro also notes that Johnson is said to have replied as follows to a Black chauffeur who told him he'd prefer to be called by name instead of "boy," "nigger" or "chief":

"As long as you are Black, and you're gonna be Black till the day you die, no one's gonna call you by your goddamn name. So, no matter what you are called, nigger, you just let it roll off your back like water, and you will make it. Just pretend you are a god damn piece of furniture."

The following quote is from "The Iron Triangle" by Vance Everett Ellison

On April 16, 2019, when speaking about congressional districts with large minority populations Speaker of The House Nancy Pelosi triumphantly stated, while sipping a glass of water "This glass of water would win with a D next to its name in those districts." To say this so arrogantly without any fear of repercussion is clear evidence that the Democrats believe they have control of what Lyndon Johnson described as "them Niggers."

Many government calculations analysis data reports released by many groups show that despite nearly **$22 trillion** in total welfare spending since President Lyndon Johnson began the "war on poverty" in 1964, the poverty rate in the United States has remained relatively constant.

Since 1967, the Democrats have overseen more than two dozen inner cities. Most mayors and police chiefs were Black people, and most Northern states governors were from the Democratic party. Then why are Black economic conditions and social order today almost the same as it was under slavery before emancipation? What happened to the 22 trillion dollars? The Democrats think that money is the solution for all the problems. The Black community can only advance after they embrace some social values. The fundamental issue is fatherlessness. It is an intergenerational curse. The Black families and their churches should stop the demonization of the White race and victimhood. Even more than 90 percent of Black pastors support the Democratic party. They sold their soul to the devil for the sake of color.

There are stark similarities between today's Blacks and the Blacks during slavery.

One example is broken down and dilapidated buildings. Today, just visit the inner cities of the Democratic controlled cities and you will witness it. Another similarity is broken down families. It is really hard to identify the fathers.

In addition, there was unceasing violence. Barbed wire fences, beatings by slave-overseers, and police brutality were daily events. Today, in addition to the gun violence, other violences take place, however, the media doesn't cover them. Since it is a daily occurrence, the media is not interested in reporting it. However, the media will broadcast 24 hours a day, if White police kill a Black man. I am providing one statistic concerning Chicago: In 2022, the crime rate was lower compared to the previous years. The reader can make a logical evaluation.

"Chicago has topped 600 homicides and 2,600 shootings in 2022, according to new Chicago Police Department data. Though both of those totals mark double-digit declines over each of the past two years, they remain above pre-pandemic levels."

By the end of November, 3,258 people have been shot in the city, according to monthly crime stats from the CPD. Of those victims, 637 people were killed. The number of homicides represents a

15% decline compared to the same time in 2021.

The number of shootings recorded so far this year (2,647) is also down nearly 20% over last year.

"Our officers are out in the community working to keep others safe and I want to thank them for upholding the mission to serve and protect," Police Superintendent David Brown said.

During slavery, the slaves received basic food and medical care to sustain life so that they would be healthy enough to perform hard labor. Today, they get free healthcare under Medicaid, along with food stamps and other provisions. No one gets ahead in life. Most of the young Black's dropout from school. The Democrats at that time called slavery a school of civilization. Pessimism, despair, anger, and rebellion are an intergenerational curse which have become their lifestyle.

So, the Democratic party convinced others that only government could provide the answer to the problems that plagued Black Americans. This can be considered as the modern-day Democratic plantation.

The Democratic Party has molded most

Black Americans, as the Czar molded the Russians and the Emperor molded the Chinese, to fit the model of their greatest asset: the compliant and obedient servant. This model has existed from antiquity. Since the 1800's Black Americans are the property under the control of White Democrats. Liberalism cannot survive in America without Black support. Today's reparation movement is from a spirit of unforgiveness. Black people are the only Americans forbidden to evolve and are instead pushed to devolve.

Stockholm Syndrome and American Blacks

Or

The Willie Lynch Syndrome

The Cleveland Clinic describes the Stockholm syndrome as:

"A coping mechanism to a captive or abusive situation. People develop positive feelings toward their captors or abusers over time. This condition applies to situations including child abuse, coach-athlete abuse, relationship abuse and sex trafficking. Treatment includes psychotherapy ("talk therapy") and medications if needed."

Overview

What is Stockholm Syndrome?

Stockholm syndrome is a psychological response to being held captive. People with Stockholm syndrome form a psychological connection with their captors and begin sympathizing with them.

In addition to the original kidnapper-hostage situation, Stockholm syndrome now includes other types of traumas in which there's a bond between the abuser and the person being abused.

Many medical professionals consider the victim's positive feelings toward their abuser a psychological response — a coping mechanism — that they use to survive the days, weeks or even years of trauma or abuse.

Other closely linked psychological conditions include:

- Trauma bonding
- Learned helplessness
- Battered person syndrome

The Willie Lynch Syndrome

Vince Everett Ellison in his book, 'The Iron Triangle' provides a cogent explanation:

"Democratic control of the Black community in the twenty-first century is a continuation of the mind control phenomenon called the "Willie Lynch syndrome." This phenomenon was designed and mastered by slave master extraordinaire Willie Lynch. It is "Stockholm Syndrome" by another name and is explained in excerpts taken from his speech given on the banks of the James River in 1712 called, "The Making of a Slave."

Here are some excerpts: "I greet you here on the bank of the James River in the year of our Lord one Thousand Seven Hundred and Twelve. First, I shall thank you, the gentlemen of the Colony of Virginia, for bringing me here. I am here to help you to solve some of your problems with slaves. Your invitation reached me on my modest plantation in the West Indies, where I have experimented with some of the newest and still oldest methods of control of the slaves. I have a foolproof method of controlling your Black slaves. I guarantee every one of you that if installed correctly it will control the slaves for at least **three hundred years.**

"It is necessary that your slaves trust and depend on us. They must love, respect and trust only us. Whereas nature provides them with the natural capacity to take of their offspring, we break that natural string of independence from them thereby creating a dependency status, so that we may be able to get from them useful production for our business and pleasure.

"When it comes to breaking the uncivilized nigger. Take the meanest and most restless nigger, strip him of his clothes in front of the remaining male niggers, the females, and the nigger infants, tar and feather him, tie each leg to a different horse faced in opposite directions, set him afire, and beat both horses to pull him apart in front of the remaining niggers. The next step is to take a bull whip and beat the remaining nigger male to a point of death, in front of the female and the infant. Don't kill him. Put the fear of God in him, for he can be useful for future breeding.

"Take the female: if she shows any sign of resistance in submitting completely to your will, do not hesitate to use the bullwhip on her to exact that last bit of resistance out of her. When in complete submission, she will train her offspring in the early years to submit to labor, when they become of age.

By her being left alone, unprotected, with the male image destroyed, the ordeal caused her to move from her psychological dependent state to a frozen independent state. In this frozen state of independence, she will raise her male and female offspring in reversed roles. For fear of the young male's life, she will train him to be mentally weak and dependent, but physically strong."

Now you know why most Blacks vote for the Democratic party.

5

Is Systemic Racism Existing In America?

Merriam-Webster's current definition of racism

1. A belief that races is the primary determinant of human traits and capacities and that racial differences produce an inherent superiority of a particular race

2. a) a doctrine or political program based on the assumption of racism and designed to execute its principles, b) a political or social system founded on racism

3. racial prejudice or discrimination

According to my interpretation: **"Anyone on the globe who blames America for racism is incorrigibly jealous, unjust, racist, and ignorant."**

Romans 3:11-18 states:

"There is no one righteous, not even one there is no one who understands; there is no one who seeks God. All have turned away, they have together become worthless; there is no one who does good, not even one. Their throats are open graves; their tongues practice deceit." The poison of vipers is on their lips. Their mouths are full of cursing and bitterness. Their feet are swift to shed blood; ruin and misery mark their ways, and the way of peace they do not know. There is no fear of God before their eyes."

No nation or people can claim moral superiority ever since the creation.

America is not exempt from sin and injustice.

Many in the world consider slavery as the original sin of America without any redemption and the present-day White race must be punished. History books all over the world followed some early historian's false narratives and the true history is buried. Why does everyone demonize slavery in the USA? Why is no one discussing the slavery in the Middle east especially in Egypt, Saudi Arabia, and Syria. Why does no one discuss slavery in South America? **It is estimated that as many as eleven million Africans were transported across the Atlantic. Ninety-five percent of which went to South and Central America, mainly to Portuguese, Spanish and French possessions. Only 5 percent of the slaves went to the United States.**

However, at least 28 million Africans were enslaved in the Muslim Middle East. At least 80 percent of those captured by Muslim slave traders were calculated to have died before reaching the slave markets. It is believed that the death toll from the 14 centuries of Muslim slave trade into Africa could have been 112 million. When added to the number of those sold in the slave markets, the total number of African victims of the Trans Saharan and East African slave trade could be around 140 million.

While most slaves who went to America could marry and have families, most of the male slaves destined for the Middle East slave bazaars were castrated and most of the children born to the women from them were killed at birth because Muslim men did not want to raise children from a slave woman. Imagine the gruesome scenes, before medical revolution in the primitive time; a knife is used without anesthesia for castrating men. Comparing the slaves in India and Africa, American slavery was more humane.

A comparison of the Islamic slave trade to the American slave trade reveals some interesting contrasts. While two out of every three slaves shipped across the Atlantic were men, the proportions were reversed in the Islamic slave trade. Two women for every man were enslaved by the Muslims. While the mortality rate for slaves being transported across the Atlantic was as high as 10%, the percentage of slaves dying in transit in the Trans Sahara and East African slave trade was between 80 and 90%.

While almost all the slaves shipped across the Atlantic were for agricultural work, most of the slaves destined for the Muslim Middle East were for sexual exploitation as concubines, in harems, and for military service. Many children were born to slaves in the Americas, and millions of their descendants are citizens in the USA to this day. The descendants under Islamic nations are very few or do not exist. In the USA, the Black population is 14.6% of the total population. America even elected a Black president and many blacks are serving in prominent places in the USA.

American slavery was a small percentage of the slavery that took place throughout the universe. Although American slaves suffered, it benefited the descendants of them in America. American Blacks are better off than any other Black people in the world.

However, in other countries, slaves have no descendants because they perished without leaving any children. In the Middle East today you do not see any Black population like there is in the USA.

America recognized her past sins and apologized and rectified its errors. Have you seen the President of Egypt or Syria and king of Saudi Arabia apologize for exterminating the Black population? Also have you read about the president of Brazil, Argentina and other Latin American countries apologizing for their past sins? The whole world knows that it can scare the liberal and Godless White man. Additionally, the Black population has an exempt status from many inflammatory and racist comments. Perfect examples are the rioting, looting, and burning down by BLM and Antifa in two dozen cities. Most of them did not face any consequences. My question is why does everyone in the world debate and discuss only American slavery? I see an international racism against America.

There is No Systemic Racism in America

By Gabrielle Seunagal

June 11, 2020

For quite some time now, Democrats have force-fed a false narrative to Americans. That false narrative asserts that the United States is just overflowing with supposed "systemic racism."

The Fallacy of "Systemic Racism"

Similarly, to "White privilege," "systemic racism" is a lie crafted by the Democrats in order to advance their political power. For the political left to remain relevant, they need a part of the population to feel oppressed, victimized, and burdened. There is no better way of doing this than by deceiving people into believing that "the system" is out to get them.

The United States of America is the greatest nation in the world. It is a land of opportunity, and people of all races can succeed and make something of themselves. Leftists loathe hearing this because it flies in the face of the narrative asserting inescapable Black/minority victimhood.

Individualism vs. Collectivism

Telling entire groups of people that their skin color is a handicap is wrong and malicious. However, individuals who internalize this fallacy can sadly transform it into a negative, self-fulfilling prophecy. People who internalize the false narrative that "the system" is out to get them are more likely to have a different mindset than those who haven't bought into this sham.

Prisons in America

Black Americans are incarcerated in state prisons at nearly five times the rate of White Americans, according to a new report by The Sentencing Project.

The report found that one in 81 Black adults per 100,000 people in the United States are serving time in a state prison, using data and projections from recent years from the US Census, the US Bureau of Justice Statistics, and information provided directly from some states.

Frequently, American television channels, radio, and newspapers cry foul with American judicial system where Blacks are disproportionately arrested and jailed. American Black population comprise between 13 to 14 percent of the total population. However, a higher percentage of Blacks are in jail. Hypothetically, imagine if America adopted the liberal remedies and established a utopian society. Blacks would be in jail at the same rate as before. Liberals are looking into wrong places for remedies. Instead of brainwashing from childhood hatred against America and White men, the Black race must transform their culture completely. Why are 250,000 people per month from 150 countries trying to enter America? If America is so bad, no one would come here. People all over the world know inside their heart that Americans are better than anyone else in the world. Two Indian origin Americans have declared their candidacy for the 2024 American presidential election. One is Nikkei Haley and the other is Vivek Ramaswamy. Today, India origin Kamala Harris is the vice president. Rishi Sunak is the prime minister of Great Britain.

Today, just examine the condition all over the world. Hindu fanatics in India are attacking and burning down Christian Churches in many parts of North India. Christians are being killed in most Islamic countries, especially in Nigeria. Can any sober person claim that Indians, Blacks, and other races are better than the White race? If anyone feels so they should cross the border of those counties for an experimental purpose. If the Black race was in power, they would suppress all others. We can see their DNA in BLM and Antifa riots. It is hard for a South Indian to have prominence in Indian politics.

Just watch the evening news in every city. Most crimes are conducted by Black people. If you are a truth seeker, you can get all the data from the government. In America, millions of immigrants are living without any issues. Blacks from Nigeria, Congo, Burkina Faso, Rwanda, and the Caribbean islands, as well as Indian, Chinese, Vietnamese, Japanese, and Korean people are living in peace. They do not face police brutality because they do not fight with police. Have you ever thought why a Black immigrant from Nigeria or an Indian immigrant is shot by the police? Because our culture taught us to obey the police command not to fight with them. There are bad police officers everywhere, and it is the duty of the local government to hire, good police force, and train them to be humane. Although the Democrats controlled all the branches of the government for decades, why does systemic racism exist in America? The liberals rule most states, universities, and media. If racism continue to exist, liberals are solely responsible for it.

School system

In the past, Democratic leaders stood in the doorways of schoolhouses and told Black school children that "we don't want you in here to receive good education that our children are getting." Today, many Black students have become mired in urban schools that are often failing or deteriorating, Democrats are once again standing in the doorway, this time to keep Black students from getting out. It proves that for one-and-a-half centuries, Democrats have taken wrong positions on educational opportunities for Black students.

Black students get suspended from school more than other kids. According to liberal ideology, this must be because they are discriminated against.

But the simple fact is that Black students commit more violent offences in public schools than other kids.

John McWhorter in his book, "Woke Racism" explains: "The Philadelphia Inquirer fanned out across the city's public schools in 2012 and found out that there had been thirty thousand violent incidents in public schools between 2007 and then, which included robberies, rapes, and a pregnant teacher punched in the stomach. (She was one of four thousand teachers assaulted by students between 2005 and 2010.)"

If anyone points out the high Black crime rate, the liberals call it racism. White politicians who wore black face makeup as a joke faced intense criticisms. At the same time Black politicians and leaders have a blanket immunity from any racist acts. Furthermore, they have great immunity in American society. Black journalist Nikole Hannah Jones stated that the Revolutionary War was fought to preserve slavery. She got a Pulitzer for it. Also, Ta-Nehisi Coats a Black writer stated that the September 11 bombing was justified and White people deserved to die.

"Between the World and Me" (2015), won the National Book Award for nonfiction by Ta-Nehisi Coates. This book was required reading for millions of undergraduates nationwide for years. He stated that he had no sympathy for the White cops and firemen who died at the World Trade Center on September 11, 2001. They were just "menaces of nature; they were the fire, the comet, the storm, which could- with no justification-shatter my body."

No wonder Ronald Regan said, "Liberalism is a mental disorder." If this racist evil writer lived in Africa or any other nation, he would not have seen the next day's sunlight. Then he would understand true racism.

What is the Solution for Black America?

A real Black leader must arise in the Black community and dismantle the structures of its culture and lifestyle. Do not brainwash their children with hatred and victimhood. Instill good Christian values. The nation of Islam and others teach that Christianity is a White man's religion. Many Blacks are converted to Islam in jail. The number is staggering. The American Blacks have no clue that Islam despise blackness and Black people. Hadith clearly states that Muhammad is a White man. According to the translation of Sura 3:106-107 from the Arabic version, on judgment day, only people with white faces will be saved. Islamic paradise promises 72 White virgins for the faithful. There for anyone in prison hear some selected narrations from Koran and accept Islam it would be a great disaster. On death they will have a rude awakening. Many American Blacks have fallen in this trap.

Let me conclude with Galatians 3:28-29 NLT translation.

"There is no longer Jew or Gentile slave or free, male, and female. For you are all one in Christ Jesus. And now that you belong to Christ, you are the true children of Abraham. You are his heirs, and God's promise to Abraham belongs to you."

If you enjoyed this book, consider the following books by the same author:

Christians and Politics

DR. SUNNY EZHUMATTOOR
(DR. JOHN MATHEW)

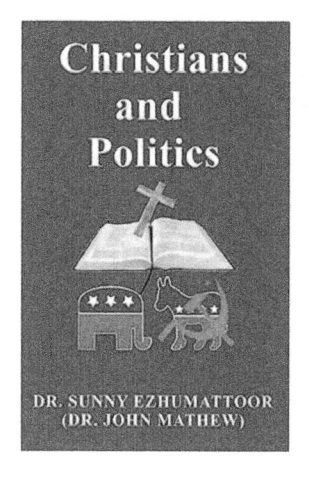

Available on Amazon

    Every generation must make a renewed defense of the true Gospel, because the Gospel is under attack in each successive generation. Wokeness, Transgenderism, and CRT are destroying the Christian foundation of America. The new idea is basically neo-Marxism for deconstruction and dismantling of Social and economic structures of the West. They have invented new vocabulary like systemic racism, implicit bias, whiteness, white privilege, cultural appropriation, colonization, microaggression, equity and social justice.

The Malaise of the Malayalees

DR. SUNNY EZHUMATTOOR

Available on Amazon

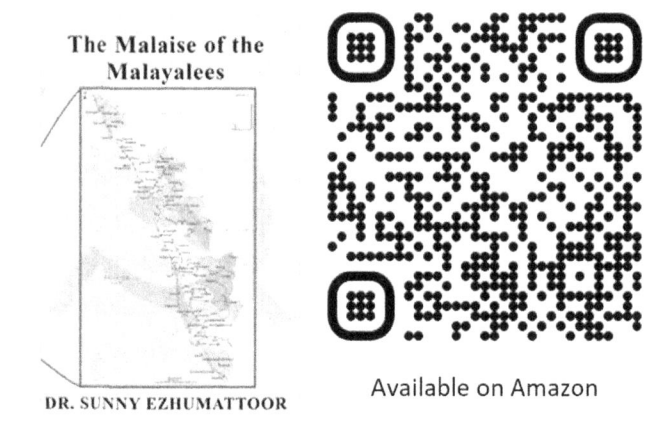

Dr. John Mathew who is also known Dr. Sunny Ezhumattoor , author of many excellent books on Amazon ...good bible teacher , wider understanding of current affairs, in short , he is kind of encyclopedia to ask any question ...he has an answer ...my curiosity always not much biblical but more sociological and often I have raised questions related to Kerala and Christian and their practices, these all were in my thought persevered it during my three years of study in Kerala, i did not find any one to answer me, most don't like to response to a non-Malayalee like me, covering each other is common syndrome among this community... But he always responded to me with a lengthy answer with many other facts I was not aware of.

Sabir Ali
Banglore

Available on Amazon

Orde Wingate was the founder of the Modern Israel army. He is the father of modern warfare. He believed the Biblical prophecies regarding Israel in the Bible. He was born and brought up in a Plymouth Brethren family in Scotland. He was born and died in India.

The Brethren Movement

Powerscourt Castle

DR JOHN MATHEW

Available on Amazon

The history, doctrine, and practices of the Plymouth Brethren. An overview of the distinctive s of the Brethren Assemblies.

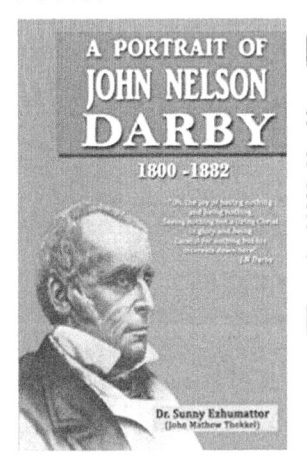

A PORTRAIT OF JOHN NELSON DARBY 1800 -1882

Dr. Sunny Ezhumattor
(John Mathew Thekkel)

Available on Amazon

Contribution of John Nelson Darby in shaping American fundamentalism and the Republican Party. History of Pre-Tribulation Rapture and Bible Translation. Brief biographies of great men like George Muller and Sir Robert Anderson. History of Antisemitism.

Available on Amazon

What is called "falling out in the spirit," "holy laughter" and the wild jerking and body gyration that is so dominant in many churches today, should be judged based on what the Scriptures teach and what is changed in the lives of the individuals? It should never be borrowed from some false religion. There are accounts of worship, where David danced before the Lord and the healed a man in Acts three, walking, leaping and praising God, but the individual was always reverential with great awe before the Lord. Did God ever instruct David to worship Him with all instruments and loud voice and dance? Did David ask the Lord or any prophets about the appropriateness of this type of worship?

Available on Amazon

The role and purpose of the Holy Spirit has been one of great misunderstandings among Christians since the first century. In this book, Dr. Sunny Ezhumattoor (a Bible scholar, historian, and researcher) answers most of the questions concerning this matter with relevance to the Holy Bible. This is an appropriate study for students and researchers of this controversial subject.

Available on Amazon

Available on Amazon

Available on Amazon

**Sovereignty
and
Limited
~~Atonement~~**
Free Will

DR JOHN MATHEW

Available on Amazon

     This work is to rescue true believers from the shackles of five-point Calvinism and about the power and plan of God for the world. My goal is not to debate the five points of Calvinism, but to point out some serious errors and misconceptions believed by Calvinists. While following a few pro Calvinist websites through Facebook, one truth became evident to me: the ardent followers of Calvinism are following a cult.

Available on Amazon

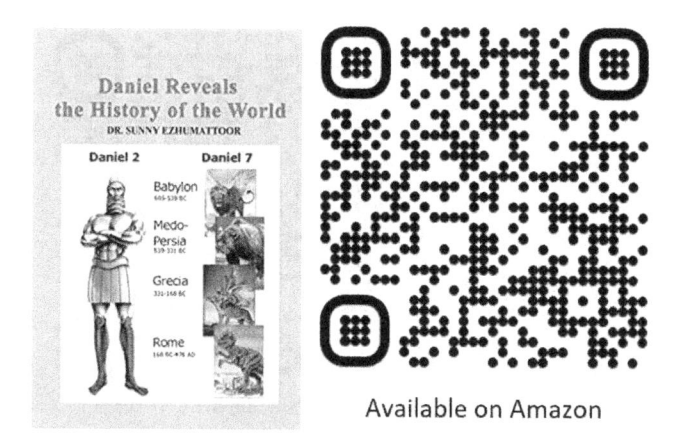

Daniel was a mouthpiece of God, and by revelation, he interpreted King Nebuchadnezzar's dream about the destinies of the earth's kingdoms, and the kingdom of God that would never pass away. He also prophesied about Christ's death, and the events that would lead to His return. As a leading authority on many subjects, Dr. John Mathew has dedicated many years to the study of Biblical prophecies and world events. Holding degrees in History, Law, and Theology, Dr. Mathew tackles day-to-day subjects with accuracy, clarity, and a pragmatic approach. His emphasis on current issues has been the hallmark of his writings. This study book, Daniel Reveals the History of the World, can transform you by integrating world events with historical prophecies, and expanding on difficult passages to provide a unique perspective.

Available on Amazon

      This book on Revelation is written for a twenty first Century reader. The events in the book of Revelation are connected with current events in the world. This book explains the chronological order of the Third World War.

Available on Amazon

      This book contains spiritual principles for a person from birth to death. The roles of the husband, wife, father, mother, son, daughter, and grandparents are given in cogent fashion based on the Bible.

Bibliography

Rules for Radicals
    Alinksy, Saul

American History in Black & White
    Barton, David

    Moore, Stephen

The Climate Chronicles
    Bastardi, Joe

Hot Talk, Cold Science
    Clarke, Arthur

The Iron Triangle
    Ellison, Vince Everett

Politics According to the Bible
    Grudem, Wayne

Final Battle
    Horowitz, David

Who Are We?
    Huntington, Samuel

Killing For God
    Kamble, Paul

Fundamentals Of Dialectical Materialism
Edited by G. Kursanov
Progress Publishers, Moscow

American Marxism
Levin, Mark

We Will Not Be Silenced
Lutzer, Erwin

Is God On America's Side?
Lutzer. Erwin

Manifesto of the Communist Party
Marx, Karl, and Engels, Frederick. Moscow> progress Publishers, 1965

It's Ok to Leave the Plantation
Mason, Clarence

Conspiracy Theories
Ezhumattoor, Sunny

Betrayed Black America
McWhorter, John

Threats of Doom
Moore, Patrick

2006 Atlantic Hurricane Season; Follow
> *Moore, Stephen*

the (Climate Change) Money, Dec.18,2018 (Imprimis)

Fundamentals of Scientific Socialism, Trans. G. Ivanov- Mujiev, Union of Soviet Republics, 1969.

The War On The west
> *Murray, Douglas*

Nineteen Eighty-Four
> *Orwell, George*

Woke, Inc
> *Ramaswamy, Vivek*

"Reagan's Moral Courage." Imprimis, 40,Nov.11(2011)
> *Roberts, Andrew*

Race And Culture
> *Sowell, Thomas*

Blacks Rednecks and White Liberals
> *Sowell, Thomas*

Christianity And Wokeness
> *Strachan, Owen*

Capitalism A Panacea For Socio- Economic Woes
Thekkel, Mathew

Race & Economics, How Much Can Be Blamed on Discrimination?
Williams, Walter Hoover institution Press,2011

Liberty Versus the Tyranny of Socialism, Essays 2208
William Walter

Black Masters
Wilson, Calvin Dill

Made in the USA
Middletown, DE
01 September 2023